Mud : Home, Body And Me

A Journey from Womb to Self

Pooja Mishra

India | USA | UK

Copyright © Pooja Mishra
All Rights Reserved.

This book has been self-published with all reasonable efforts taken to make the material error-free by the author. No part of this book shall be used, reproduced in any manner whatsoever without written permission from the author, except in the case of brief quotations embodied in critical articles and reviews.

The Author of this book is solely responsible and liable for its content including but not limited to the views, representations, descriptions, statements, information, opinions, and references ["Content"]. The Content of this book shall not constitute or be construed or deemed to reflect the opinion or expression of the Publisher or Editor. Neither the Publisher nor Editor endorse or approve the Content of this book or guarantee the reliability, accuracy, or completeness of the Content published herein and do not make any representations or warranties of any kind, express or implied, including but not limited to the implied warranties of merchantability, fitness for a particular purpose.

The Publisher and Editor shall not be liable whatsoever...

Made with ❤ on the BookLeaf Publishing Platform
www.bookleafpub.in
www.bookleafpub.com

Dedication

Dedicated to my mother.
For giving me my first home, nurturing my body and
shaping the woman I am today.
Your love is the mud from which I grew.

Preface

Life begins in a humble, dark, unseen place—a space both safe and mysterious. In these pages, I explore that space: the womb, the first home, and the journey of becoming. This collection traces a girl's path from the comfort of her earliest beginnings to the vast, complex world outside. It is about learning from home, from the body, and from life itself.

Each poem is a step, a reflection, and a celebration of discovery: the wonder of growing, the lessons of living, and the realization of self.

I invite you to walk this path with me, to feel the mud beneath your feet, the warmth of home around you, and the rhythm of your own becoming.

Acknowledgements

This book is a reflection of every hand, heart, and moment that shaped me.

I am deeply grateful to my family for their love, patience, and unwavering faith — you have been my anchor and my light through every season of change.

A special thanks to my husband, whose quiet strength and constant belief have gently pushed me toward my dreams. Your support has been the calm beneath my chaos, the reason I could keep going.

To the women — past, present, and within — who taught me the strength of softness and the beauty of becoming,
And to life itself, for moulding me through every shade of mud and light —
this book is for you.

1. Part I - Mud in Body : Seeded in Hope

Her womb was the mud,
Where I was seeded with hope.
She gave me her blood,
So that I could learn the art of love.

I was nurtured in my mother's embrace,
Pampered with care, warmth, and nourishment.
I believe I ripened perfectly that day,
To grow into who and what I am today.

2. Heartbeats and Tiny Laughters

I was a tiny gift from God, the answer to her prayers,
Beating within her, free from all worries and fears.
She gave me the sense of joy and emotion,
I felt her moods, even without words or motion.
I never knew when we formed this deep connection —
A bond of love, beyond all comprehension.
She talked to me when no one was around,
And I wished I could smile back at her tiny laughs of sound.

3. Growing with Her

I was growing, sensing, developing each day,
The mud of my body shaping its way.

Why she cried, I could not understand,
For I was a little heart with only a little mind.

I giggled, I smiled whenever she was fine,
My little heart leapt with her joys divine.
Safe always inside her body, I lay,
She was the only hero
In the story of mine.

4. First Kick

Today, I kicked her for the very first time,
She gasped in wonder, her face lit with a smile.

She laughed and glowed at my tiny, wild act,
Everyone gathered, their hands traced her back.

I curled within, still dancing in delight —
Our hearts met softly in that glowing night.

5. She Knitted for Me

She knitted for me some dreams and desires,
And crafted my story — like a fish caught, cooked on fire.

There were colors, designs, and patterns to welcome me home,
Threads of love where warmth had grown.

Through her belly button, I felt her care —
A cozy touch, a silent prayer.
Her heartbeat hummed, her whispers spun,
And I knew —
my life had just begun.

6. Home Coming

Now it was time — for me to come home,
My father grew restless, his worry well known.
Wrinkles on his forehead, sweat in his hand,
Waiting for me — as time slipped like sand.

My mother was anxious, happy, and thrilled,
Her heart was racing, her eyes were filled.
Between fear and joy, she waited for me —
The world outside, ready to see.

7. Stepping into the World

My bed was carved with hope, happiness,
And tiny hails from my little sweet family.

It was the day I would meet
The people entwined with my destiny.

No wonder I was excited to emerge,
To see the new world around me.
But the moment I came out,
I realized my world always revolved
Where she was — my mother.

8. Part II - Mud in Home : The Friendly Guardian

Slowly,
Each wall, each corner held whispers of my new life.
Here, I began to feel, to notice, to sense —
The gentle warmth, the soft touch, the love surrounding me.

Sunlight streaming through the windows
Danced upon my tiny hands and feet.
Every sound, every sigh, every lullaby
Taught me comfort, safety, and the first lessons of belonging.

The rooms whispered stories I could not yet understand,
But in every embrace, every heartbeat close to mine,
It was my home.

9. Home and Growth

My home is the place that taught me so much,
Where I grew older, changing in age, place, and role.

The walls stood tall, steadfast and true,
Leaving memories where I learned to sit, speak, and crawl.

Each block of this home holds the stories of my childhood,
And how beautifully it shaped me,
Helping me embrace, celebrate, and flaunt my womanhood.

10. Walls of my Childhood

I never thought that every nook and corner
Would share pieces of my story.
The walls, the roof, the windows —
All sang of the happiness of growing old with glory.

The colours on the walls once taught me —
To greet each day like a festival,
Whether it came wrapped in laughter
Or softened by quiet tears.

Mum taught me life's lessons in this house,
I received my upbringing here,
Until the day I stepped into
My spouse's home.

11. The Base, Boundaries and the Pillars

I realised, as I was growing and glowing within my home,
That every corner held a lesson of its own.

I learnt why I must shape the four walls of my room
As equal as the boundaries of my self-respect.

I learnt the need to draw a line,
So that no negativity could seep in and affect.

I understood the strength of a pillar —
When I saw myself as a mother standing strong.
And I realised why the base must be tough —
Like the determination to endure every odd and wrong.

12. Doors and the Windows

I never realized how the silent corners of home
Could carry lessons deeper than I imagined.
Each part whispered wisdom in its own way,
And I was often surprised by what I learned.

The ceiling whispered, dream high.
The windows reminded me —
It's okay to be a little shy.

And the doors, they taught me control —
To draw a line, to decide
Whom to let in,
For the peace of my mind and soul.

13. The Courtyard Tree

There was an old tree in the courtyard —
My sibling, my friend,
My watchman, my bodyguard.

I used to share all my little happenings
With the tree I had named my own.

It was my only companion —
The silent witness to my mischief,
My happiness, and my cries.

I buried my pain deep beneath its roots,
Hoping the grass would grow above,
And set my heart free.

14. The Old Trunk

There was an old trunk kept in the corner of the store,
And it was always fun to open and explore.

Inside were memories safely preserved by my mother,
Holding years of love, pain, successes, and failures.

Little mirrors, colourful ribbons, Mom's belongings,
And the clothes of all family members.

How much there was to cherish when it was opened,
And how much it revealed about sentiment and perseverance.

Each time I lift its lid, I find something new —
Reminding me that memories never age, they just renew.

15. The Mirror on the Wall

Few things can't replace our lifestyle,
Yet they can bring back a long-lost smile.

The big, old mirror — still hanging on the wall —
Had watched me grow,
Flaunting my flaws since the time I learned to crawl.

Mom's bindi, her lipstick, her comb —
They always filled my world with fantasy.
I looked so beautiful wearing her ornaments and jewellery,
As if I were the reflection she once used to be.

The mirror taught me to stay beautiful
Even on the hardest of days.
It told me never to lose hope
And to be confident in every possible way.

I learned to wipe the dust from its surface
To see my face clearly —

Just as I must clear the negativities of my soul
To keep shining through life's race.

16. The Temple

There is a small wooden temple in my home —
Firm, calm, and beautifully carved,
Adorned with pictures and statues
Of many Gods and Goddesses.

Mom always taught me how to keep my faith alive —
To light a diya even when life faces its toughest odds.

Meditating there helped me learn
How to stay focused on life's purpose and goal.

I learned that keeping faith in something invisible
Is never easy to sustain.

But those who rise above doubt and failure,
Who take accountability for their actions,
Are the ones who truly embrace happiness —
Seeing the rainbow instead of the rain.

17. Part III - Mud in Me : The Moulding Self

The mud in me never settled down —
It was bruised, cut, and polished
Until I reached my womanhood crown.

The journey of what I am today
Was never as easy as it seems.
I had to learn a lesson at every step
To let my soul heal and dream.

Little wonder, crazy teen, or multitasking woman I've been —
Judged at every phase,
As people kept wondering
Why the other side of the grass looked always green.

I kept working with a heart full of fears,
For I was the princess of my mom —
How could I ever bring her to tears?

18. Shades of Me

The story began with a tiny girl,
Standing tall with curls and rolls.

A round face, a little nose,
Soft lips, curious eyes.

I was a copy of my dad —
Dashing, wise, and full of charm.
I carried some brown from my mom,
For which she was taunted by narrow minds:

"Oh, pity girl! So dark in complexion!
Who will marry her and give her love?"

I was too small to understand
These words, these arrows.
I often wondered
How my parents tackled such cruelty
With patience, love, and quiet strength.

19. Becoming

I grew a little more with grace,
Felt new changes on my body and face.

Something within began to turn —
A rhythm I didn't yet discern.
I wasn't ready for what had begun,
Unsure if I should hide or run.

It started one day, quiet and strange,
A mark of life, a sign of change.

I wasn't accepting my body that day,
But feared the gossips that came my way.
A little ashamed, a little scared,
I burst into tears, unprepared.

At school, I sat in silent fear —
No one around to calm or hear.
My heart kept racing, wild and shy,
As I wished the day would pass me by.

20. Mother's Door

I came back home with teary eyes,
Thinking I'd made some mistake of mine.

Mom opened the door — I ran to her side,
Hugged her tightly and sat down to cry.

I was shivering with fear, drenched in sweat,
My body uneasy, my mind upset.

The curious mind was settled and calm,
With hot drinks and chocolates from Mom.
She made me see nature's miracle clear —
That nothing was wrong, there's nothing to fear.

21. The First Bloom

Curves began to shape my skin,
Quietly, softly, deep within.
I tried to hide what nature gave,
Afraid of the gazes I couldn't brave.

I cursed myself, I questioned God,
For all the pains the girls endure.
Why must we bear what we never asked,
And face the world so unsure?

"Nature gifts this only to a woman,"
Mom said, to soothe my mind and heart.
I wiped my tears and looked into her eyes,
Listening to her words with awe and surprise.

22. Flow of Courage

She continued with her words,
Each wrapped in love and care,
To heal my body and soul.

"Oh dear,
This isn't just a simple blood flow —
It's nature's way
To let impurities go.

It's the courage
That flows from a mother's womb
To her daughter,
Through the umbilical cord.

It's beauty —
Sharpened through dead skin and flaws,
A reminder that even pain
Has its noble cause.

You are the one

Who will rise and roar.
When it comes to your body,
Make it a truth you're sure to adore."

23. Part IV - The Fired Clay: From Heat to Harmony

They placed me in the furnace of expectations,
Molded by hands that meant well but pressed too tight.
Every crack, every burn taught me resilience —
I learned to shine, not despite the heat, but because of it.

Through the flames of judgment and duty,
I found the rhythm of patience and strength.
The fire that could have broken me
Became the reason I could bend without falling.

From the heat that shaped me,
A quiet rhythm began to start —
The voice of courage, the questioning heart.

24. The Questioning Heart

I began asking why more than how,
Why should I always listen, always bow?

Why my laughter must hide behind grace,
Why rules are drawn just for my space?

The mirror showed a girl half-grown,
With dreams she feared to call her own.

I wanted to run, to dance, to fly —
Yet was told, "A good girl never tries."

Between the lines of right and wrong,
I searched for a place where I belong.

I struggled, I screamed, I questioned the wrong,
The societal norms always gave me blisters.
But my family stood by me, supporting my dreams,
Giving me strength to grow beyond their whispers.

25. Whispers of the World

With each growing year,
I was expected to fit
Into the narrow frame of society —
Dressing, speaking, even walking,
Measured by what was "good" or "bad,"
As they forced me into the name of a "good girl."

I cut my hair like any boy,
Hid my femininity behind clothes like theirs.
I struggled to prove myself in academics and sports,
Yet every time, I was judged for being a woman.

I never distinguished between pink and blue —
Then why did they limit my choices to just a few?

I struggled, I screamed, I questioned the wrong,
Society's norms always left me with blisters long.

But my family stood by me,

Supporting my dreams,
Giving me strength to rise above the whispers.

26. Scars and Stars

Growing up was never easy for me as a girl,
It felt like a roller-coaster — full of slides and twirls.

Yet, I never lost hope while running life's race,
Even when bruises and scars marked my face.

They said, "This isn't your field to conquer or excel,"
And laughed each time I stumbled or fell.

But little did they know, their words were my fire —
Each failure a spark, lifting me higher.

Each fall left its mark, each doubt left a scar,
Yet every bruise taught me how strong we are.
I learned to rise, to stand, to fight,
To turn my darkness into light.

The world once laughed at my trembling pace,
Now I meet it with courage, poise, and grace.

The scars and bruises tell my story true,
Of a girl who fell, then reached for the stars too.

27. Hands and Wings

I was the elder daughter in the family,
Full of grace, responsibilities,
And a heart brimming with dreams and desires.

I studied, played, danced, and worked hard,
Earning medals, trophies, and scholarships to hone my path.

Burdened under the "good girl" image, I tried to fly,
Though my wings were broken, I never let myself cry.

Later, I married and became a mother,
Restarting my career in a place entirely new.

Juggling multiple roles, I smiled with pride,
I worked, I cooked, I cared for my child.
Yet when my second baby was too small to be alone,
I left my job, to nurture life at home.

Still, deep within, my wings stirred and whispered,

Of dreams and desires that were never to be withered.
In quiet moments, I let them spread,
Remembering the girl I once had led.

I learned to balance hands and wings,
To care, to nurture, yet chase my own things.
Motherhood, marriage, work — they shape my days,
But my spirit soars in its own graceful ways.

Now I hold both worlds in my palm and heart,
Each responsibility a part of my art.
And with my wings, I reach for the skies,
A woman complete, yet still ready to rise.

28. Echoes of Me

In the quiet corners of my mind, I hear whispers —
echoes of me,
Shaped by laughter, tears, and all that I've dared to be.

I have no regrets for what I left behind,
Nor for what I longed to become.

God has His own plan for each of us,
And amidst the chaos, we must strengthen that trust.

No matter what, I will reach what I am destined for;
I might need a pause,
But the prayers of my loved ones
Can never be denied.

These echoes guide me,
Soft yet steady, reminding me:
I am complete in myself,
The base of my family, reflecting my mother's strength.

I have learned patience, calmness, tolerance,
And all the skills to face the world in my own way.

29. Crown to Self

I stand before the mirror, echoes of me in sight,
Hands steady, eyes bright, placing my crown just right.

No applause needed, no words to hear,
For I am the queen of all I hold dear.

Scars turned to wisdom, struggles into grace,
Every battle I faced has brought me to this place.

The little girl who once hid behind fear
Now smiles at the woman standing here.

Marriage and motherhood shaped my days,
Work and dreams tested my ways.
Yet I learned to balance, to rise, to see,
That strength and softness can dwell in me.

This crown is mine, forged in fire and tears,
Shining with courage earned through the years.

I honor the past, embrace what I am today,
And walk forward in my own luminous way.

30. Crown of Clay

From the seed in hope, to the kicks I felt inside,
From the walls and tree, the trunk, the mirror's guide,
Every corner of my home, every lesson learned,
Shaped the woman I am, for whom the world has turned.

Through slides and twirls, through scars and fears,
Through whispered doubts and quiet tears,
I molded my mud, I rose, I grew,
Each challenge faced, each dream pursued.

Hands that nurtured, wings that soared,
Lessons carried, love restored.
I wear my crown, not for the world to see,
But for the girl, the woman, the mother, the me.

31. Unfinished Clay

I am not yet complete —
Still shaping, still soft,
Still learning to balance strength and grace.

Every scar carries a story,
Every tear has softened my soul.
The woman I see today
Is made of patience, prayers, and quiet control.

Life has pressed, molded, and changed me,
Yet never broken my way.
I'm still being formed —
A mother, a dreamer, an unfinished clay.

32. To be Continued

This is not an ending,
Just a pause to breathe and smile.
For stories like mine
Grow deeper with every mile.

There are still corners of my heart
Waiting to be explored,
New seasons to live,
New dreams to be restored.

The mud still holds warmth,
The soul still seeks its hue —
For my journey, my crown, my story...
Will be continued too.

— Still blooming, still becoming. 🦋

A Note from the Potter

This collection began as a handful of clay —
soft, uneven, and full of stories waiting to be shaped.
With each poem, I molded fragments of my life and the world around me —
some from memory, some from moments shared, all from the heart.

Each verse carries a trace of touch — of breaking, mending, and becoming anew.
If these words found a home in your heart, perhaps they've completed their circle —
from my hands to yours, from one soul shaping to another.

With gratitude,
Pooja Mishra

www.ingramcontent.com/pod-product-compliance
Lightning Source LLC
Chambersburg PA
CBHW070039070426
42449CB00012BA/3099